Sonatinas and Easy Sonatas
for Solo Piano

31 Works by
Haydn, Mozart, Beethoven, Scarlatti,
Clementi, Dussek and Kuhlau

Selected and with an Introduction by
RONALD HERDER

DOVER PUBLICATIONS, INC.
Mineola, New York

The names Köchel, Longo, Kirkpatrick and Hoboken in a title refer to editors who catalogued, and numbered, composers' works—respectively, Ludwig von Köchel ("K"), for Mozart; Alessandro Longo ("L"), later Ralph Kirkpatrick (another "K," rarely "Kk") for Scarlatti; and Anthony van Hoboken ("Hob." or "H"), for Haydn.

Bibliographical Note

This Dover edition, first published in 1997, is a new compilation of thirty-one piano works originally published in earlier Dover and other authoritative editions. Editorial marks throughout have been retained from the original publications. Extensive editorial footnotes in the Kuhlau sonatas have been deleted.

The Dover edition adds a comprehensive list of contents, new headings throughout and an introduction specially written for this edition by Ronald Herder. We are indebted to the Wellesley College Music Library for the loan of the Dussek scores and to Seymour Bernstein for his verification of all Longo and Kirkpatrick catalog numbers.

International Standard Book Number: 0-486-29770-5

Manufactured in the United States of America
Dover Publications, Inc., 31 East 2nd Street, Mineola, N.Y. 11501

Note

The music in this collection has been the backbone of traditional piano literature for generations. It is sturdy stuff, full of attractive themes, compact development sections and resourceful solutions on a small scale. The lengths of most movements are comfortably short, giving the player a chance to learn, and perhaps memorize, a complete portion of a work in a relatively short time.

Above all, the sonatas and sonatinas in this edition are often a player's first peek into the vast world of keyboard music of the classical era—that is, of pieces composed in the 18th and early 19th centuries. Here are the great composers at their most relaxed and accessible, agreeably ready to put stormy ideas aside, to postpone complex themes and thorny materials and satisfied to ask for a lot less technique.

Simplicity is the nature of this very likeable art form, whether it is in the shape of Scarlatti's elegant one-movement dances or of Haydn's and Mozart's three-movement concert works. They are all deemed "sonatas" ("sound-pieces")—in one variation or another. The "sonatina" is a smaller, shorter member of that musical family, never too profound and content with even briefer statements.

"Easy" is a deceptive description we give to some pieces, perhaps not true all of the time. While the less complicated keys of C major and G major are favorites among these works, there is nothing simple about Mozart's "easy" Sonata in C Major, K545. Even a variant of a C major scale (and there are many of them scattered in these pages) demands respect, careful preparation and a musical approach. A good musician approaches *everything* with thoughtful care.

A good performance of one of these miniature gems will sound easy, maybe even casual. But that's another form of artistry: for nothing in this music is in itself a casual throwaway. Good composers and good poets make sure that every note, syllable, rhythm, word, phrase, sentence, dynamic and articulation is exactly in place, exactly where it should be. They hide their stylish tricks under simple robes. Our job as players is to find the riches hidden in tiny places.

Ronald Herder

Contents

Domenico Scarlatti
(Italy, 1685–1757)

Sonata in D Major
(Balletto)(L463 / K430) 2

Sonata in D Minor
(Pastorale)(L413 / K9) 4

Sonata in D Minor
(Gavotta)(L58 / K64) 6

Sonata in E Major
(Capriccio)(L23 / K380) 8

Sonata in C Major
(L104 / K159) 12

Sonata in B-flat Major
(Menuetto)(L97 / K440) 14

Sonata in F Minor
(L187 / K481) 16

Sonata in G Major
(L365 / K431) 19

Joseph Haydn
(Austria, 1732–1809)

Sonata in C Major
(Hob. No. 35)

   I. Allegro con brio 20
   II. Adagio 25
   III. *Finale:* Allegro 71

Sonata in D Major
(Hob. No. 37)

   I. Allegro con brio 30
   II. Largo e sostenuto 34
   III. *Finale:* Presto, ma non troppo 35

Sonata in G Major
(Hob. No. 40)

   I. Allegro innocente 38
   II. Presto 42

Muzio Clementi
(Italy, 1752–1832)

Six Sonatinas, Op. 36 (Complete)

No. 1 in C Major
   I. Spiritoso 45
   II. Andante 46
   III. Vivace 46

No. 2 in G Major
   I. Allegretto 48
   II. Allegretto 49
   III. Allegro 50

No. 3 in C Major
   I. Spiritoso 52
   II. Un poco adagio 54
   III. Allegro 54

No. 4 in F Major
   I. Con spirito 56
   II. Andante con espressione 58
   III. *Rondo:* Allegro vivace 59

No. 5 in G Major
   I. Presto 61
   II. *Air Suisse:* Allegro moderato 64
   III. *Rondo:* Allegro di molto 66

No. 6 in D Major
   I. Allegro con spirito 68
   II. *Rondo:* Allegretto spiritoso 72

Wolfgang Amadeus Mozart
(Austria, 1756–1791)

Sonata in C Major, K545
   I. Allegro 74
   II. Andante 77
   III. *Rondo:* Allegretto 80

JOHANN LADISLAUS DUSSEK
(Bohemia, 1760–1812)

Six Sonatinas, Op. 20 (Complete)

No. 1 in G Major
    I. Allegro non tanto   82
    II. *Rondo:* Allegretto.
    Tempo di Menuetto   84

No. 2 in C Major
    I. Allegretto quasi Andante   86
    II. *Rondo:* Non presto   88

No. 3 in F Major
    I. Allegro quasi Presto   92
    II. *Rondo:* Andantino   95

No. 4 in A Major
    I. Moderato   100
    II. *Menuetto:* Tempo di ballo   104

No. 5 in C Major
    I. Allegro moderato   106
    II. *Rondo:* Allegro moderato   107

No. 6 in E-flat Major
    I. Allegro   110
    II. *Rondo:* Allegretto   114

LUDWIG VAN BEETHOVEN
(Germany, 1770–1827)

Three Easy Sonatinas

No. 1 in C Major
    I. Allegro   117
    II. Adagio   120

No. 2 in G Major
    I. Moderato   122
    II. *Romanze* [Andantino]   123

No. 3 in F Major
    I. Allegro assai   124
    II. *Rondo:* Allegro   125

Sonata in G Minor, Op. 49, No. 1
    I. Andante   127
    II. *Rondo:* Allegro   130

Sonata in G Major, Op. 49, No. 2
    I. Allegro, ma non troppo   135
    II. Tempo di Menuetto   139

FRIEDRICH KUHLAU
(Germany, 1786–1832)

Sonatina in C Major, Op. 20, No. 1
    I. Allegro   142
    II. Andante   144
    III. *Rondo:* Allegro   145

Sonatina in C Major, Op. 55, No. 1
    I. Allegro   148
    II. Vivace   149

Sonatinas and Easy Sonatas
for Solo Piano

Sonata in D Major
(Balletto) (L463 / K430)

Domenico Scarlatti
(Italy, 1685–1757)

Non presto, ma a tempo di ballo

2

Sonata in D Minor

(Pastorale) (L413 / K9)

Domenico Scarlatti

Sonata in D Minor
(Gavotta) (L58 / K64)

Domenico Scarlatti

Sonata in E Major
(Capriccio) (L23 / K380)

Domenico Scarlatti

Sonata in C Major
(L104 / K159)

Domenico Scarlatti

Sonata in B-flat Major
(Menuetto) (L97 / K440)

Domenico Scarlatti

Sonata in F Minor

(L187 / K481)

Domenico Scarlatti

Sonata in G Major
(L365 / K431)

Domenico Scarlatti

Sonata in C Major
(Hoboken No. 35)

Joseph Haydn
(Austria, 1732–1809)

Adagio. Tempo I.

Adagio.

Finale.
Allegro.

Sonata in D Major
(Hoboken No. 37)

Joseph Haydn

Largo e sostenuto.

Attacca subito
(il) Finale.

Finale.
Presto, ma non troppo.

Innocentemente.

Sonata in G Major
(Hoboken No. 40)

Joseph Haydn

Presto.

Sonatina in C Major

(Op. 36, No. 1)

Muzio Clementi
(Italy, 1752–1832)

Spiritoso.

Sonatina in G Major
(Op. 36, No. 2)

Muzio Clementi

Sonatina in C Major
(Op. 36, No. 3)

Muzio Clementi

Sonatina in F Major
(Op. 36, No. 4)

Muzio Clementi

Andante con espressione.

Rondo

Allegro vivace

Da Capo al Fine.

Sonatina in G Major
(Op. 36, No. 5)

Muzio Clementi

Air Suisse (Original.)
Allegro moderato.

Clementi

Rondo
Allegro di molto

Sonatina in D Major

(Op. 36, No. 6)

Allegro con spirito.

Muzio Clementi

Rondo.
Allegretto spiritoso

Sonata in C Major
(K545)

Wolfgang Amadeus Mozart
(Austria, 1756–1791)

Andante.

RONDO.
Allegretto.

Sonatina in G Major

(Op. 20, No. 1)

Johann Ladislaus Dussek
(Bohemia, 1760–1812)

RONDO.
Allegretto. Tempo di Menuetto.

Minore.

Sonatina in C Major

(Op. 20, No. 2)

Johann Ladislaus Dussek

RONDO.
Non presto.

Dussek

Sonatina in F Major
(Op. 20, No. 3)

Johann Ladislaus Dussek

RONDO.
Andantino.

Maggiore.

Sonatina in A Major
(Op. 20, No. 4)

Johann Ladislaus Dussek

Moderato.

MENUETTO.
Tempo di ballo.

Fine.

D.C. al Fine.

Sonatina in C Major
(Op. 20, No. 5)

Johann Ladislaus Dussek

RONDO.
Allegro moderato.

Maggiore.

Sonatina in E-flat Major
(Op. 20, No. 6)

Johann Ladislaus Dussek

RONDO.
Allegretto.

Sonatina in C Major

No. 1 from *Three Easy Sonatinas*

Ludwig van Beethoven
(Germany, 1770–1827)

117

Adagio.

Sonatina in G Major

No. 2 from *Three Easy Sonatinas*

Ludwig van Beethoven

Moderato.

Romanze.

Sonatina in F Major

No. 3 from *Three Easy Sonatinas*

Ludwig van Beethoven

Allegro assai.

126   *Beethoven*

Sonata in G Minor
(Op. 49, No. 1)

Ludwig van Beethoven

Rondo.
Allegro.

Sonata in G Major
(Op. 49, No. 2)

Ludwig van Beethoven

Allegro, ma non troppo

Tempo di Menuetto

Sonatina in C Major
(Op. 20, No. 1)

Friedrich Kuhlau
(Germany, 1786–1832)

146   *Kuhlau*

Sonatina in C Major
(Op. 55, No. 1)

Friedrich Kuhlau

END OF EDITION